Table of Contents

Dedication..5

Appreciation...6

Chapter 1..9

- 1a. Historical Context of Jewish Education...9
- 1b. The Role of the Synagogue in Education and Community Life 11
- 1c. Jesus' Approach to Education: A Radical Departure...............11
- 1d. Scripture References to the Importance of Education and Discipleship..12
- 1e. A Model of Relational and Inclusive Discipleship....................13

Chapter 2..14

- 2a. Historical Context: The Traditional Choice of Disciples........15
- 2b. Jesus' Radical Choice of Disciples..15
- 2c. The Call to Follow: A Personal Invitation...................................16
- 2d. The Impact of Jesus' Choice: A Model for Relational Discipleship..17
- 2e. Biblical References on God's Choice of the Humble and Ordinary..18
- 2f. Jesus' Approach to Discipleship as a Model of Empowerment 19

Chapter 3..20

1

- 3a. The Historical and Cultural Significance of Modeling in Jewish Education 20
- 3b. Jesus' Approach to Modeling and the Transformative Power of Example 21
- 3c. The Influence of Jesus' Modeling on the Disciples' Character Development 22
- 3d. Biblical References Illustrating the Power of Example..........23
- 3e. The Lasting Impact of Jesus' Example on His Disciples and the Early Church 24
- 3f. Modeling as the Heart of True Discipleship 25

Chapter 4 25

- 4a. Historical and Cultural Background of Parables in Jewish Teaching 26
- 4b. The Purpose of Parables in Jesus' Ministry 27
- 4c. Key Parables and Their Significance..27
- 4d. The Role of Mystery and Revelation in Parables 29
- 4e. Parables as Invitations to Transformation 30
- 4f. The Power of Parables in Modern Discipleship........................31
- 4g. The Lasting Impact of Jesus' Parables...31

Chapter 5 32

- 5a. Historical Context: Learning Through Apprenticeship 33
- 5b. The Empowerment of the Twelve and Seventy-Two.............33
- 5c. Facing Challenges and Developing Resilience..........................34
- 5d. Biblical Examples of Empowerment in Jesus' Ministry 35

- 5e. Practical Application and the Role of the Holy Spirit............36
- 5f. The Impact of Sending Out on the Disciples' Growth..............37
- 5g. The Call to Practical Application in Modern Discipleship.....38
- 5h. Empowering Disciples to Transform the World......................39

Chapter 6..39
- 6a. The Tradition of Questioning in Jewish Culture......................40
- 6b. Jesus' Use of Questions in His Teaching..................................41
- 6c. The Power of Questions in Fostering Self-Reflection and Growth..42
- 6d. Jesus' Questions as a Means of Revelation 43
- 6e. The Role of Questions in the Disciples' Spiritual Growth.....44
- 6f. The Impact of Jesus' Questioning Method on the Early Church..44
- 6g. Application of Jesus' Questioning Method in Modern Discipleship...45

Chapter 7..47
- 7a. The Lesson of Servant Leadership 47
- 7b. Faith and Resilience in the Face of Persecution......................48
- 7c. The Promise of the Holy Spirit as a Helper and Guide..........49
- 7d. The Great Commission: A Call to Make Disciples of All Nations..50
- 7e. Love as the Defining Mark of Discipleship.................................51
- 7f. The Call to Persevere and Hold Fast to the Faith......................51

- 7g. The Power of Prayer and Dependence on God 52

Conclusion 54

Dedication

To my beloved flock at God's Pavilion, Dubai Parish.

You are more than just a congregation; you are my family, my inspiration, and my constant reminder of the beauty of discipleship. May this exploration of the Master Teacher's methods serve as a guide and encouragement as we journey together in faith, growing in wisdom, love, and purpose. This book is for you, as we strive to walk in the footsteps of Jesus, learning and serving with all our hearts.

I love you all deeply
Pastor Isaac

Appreciation

Eternal Gratitude

I am deeply grateful to those whose support, mentorship, and love have shaped my journey in ministry and personal growth.

To **Pastor Ferdinand Nnajiuba**, my Senior Pastor and Father-in-Lord, your graciousness in granting me the opportunity to lead and grow with the flock under my care has been invaluable. Thank you for trusting me with this sacred responsibility and for your encouragement every step of the way.

To **Rev. Edinam Atsutse**, your faith in me brought to light gifts and potential I could not see in myself. Thank you for nurturing these qualities to their realization, guiding me toward a deeper understanding of who I am called to be.

To **Bishop Israel Eze**, your unwavering support and mentorship have imparted lasting virtues and qualities essential to my growth as a leader. Your guidance has been a cornerstone in my journey, and I am profoundly grateful for your investment in my life.

To **Rev. Asare Offei Badu**, thank you for planting seeds of righteous Christian living in me. Your teachings and example have inspired a commitment to walking faithfully with God, and the principles you instilled continue to guide my path.

To **Rev Selorm Zeglo**, you inspired me and released the grace for me to begin to write and publish books

To **my mom, Mabel Twumasi**, and my entire family, your love and support have been a constant source of strength and encouragement. Thank you for standing by me, for your prayers, and for the sacrifices you have made for my growth.

To my siblings and extended family, thank you for your belief in me and your unwavering support. Each of you has blessed my journey, and I am profoundly grateful.

May God bless you all richly, as He has blessed me through each of you.

Introduction

The Timeless Teacher

In a world of structured education, Jesus stood out as a teacher who chose a radically different approach. His methods were not bound by classrooms, formal lectures, or academic prerequisites. Instead, He taught by living among His followers, demonstrating His lessons through actions, conversations, and everyday encounters. Jesus' approach to teaching and discipleship was deeply relational, accessible, and transformative—qualities that continue to resonate across centuries.

This book invites you to explore Jesus' unique discipleship method, examining the educational systems of His time and uncovering why He chose to teach the way He did. Each chapter delves into a core aspect of His teaching style, drawing insights that can still inspire teachers, mentors, and leaders today.

Chapter 1
Education and Discipleship in First-Century Judea

In first-century Judea, education was not widely accessible to the general population as it is today. Most people learned trades from their families, and education was generally limited to reading, memorizing, and reciting scripture in a religious setting. The focus of education for the Jewish people centered on the Torah, the first five books of the Hebrew Bible, considered foundational for understanding their identity and covenant with God.

- 1a. Historical Context of Jewish Education

In Jewish culture, formal education for boys began at around age five or six. The **Bet Sefer** (meaning "House of the Book") was the primary level of schooling where children learned to read and write Hebrew by studying the Torah. Classes were often conducted in local synagogues, where scribes or religious teachers (rabbis) would oversee their instruction. The emphasis was on memorization and oral recitation, reflecting the cultural value placed on retaining the sacred texts in memory.

For boys who excelled, around the age of ten, a secondary stage called **Bet Midrash** (meaning "House of Study") became available. In this setting, students engaged in deeper study and interpretation of the Torah, as well as other writings such as the Prophets and the Writings. They would also learn the oral traditions, which rabbis passed down through generations. The rabbis and teachers who led these studies were highly respected and typically came from established scholarly backgrounds, having trained under other rabbis themselves.

By the time a young man reached his early teens, only the most talented and dedicated continued on this path. The brightest students might seek to follow a rabbi full-time, learning through observation and practice, similar to an apprenticeship. This process of becoming a rabbi's disciple was intense, often involving a commitment to study, emulate, and even adopt the lifestyle and character of their teacher. This kind of relationship is seen in the New Testament, where Paul speaks of being trained by Gamaliel, a renowned rabbi (Acts 22:3).

- **1b. The Role of the Synagogue in Education and Community Life**

The synagogue was not only a place of worship but also a community center for education, legal discussions, and social gatherings. Jesus Himself often taught in synagogues (Luke 4:16-21) and used these spaces to explain His teachings and reveal His identity. For example, in Nazareth, He reads from the scroll of Isaiah in the synagogue and announces the fulfillment of this prophecy through Himself (Luke 4:18-21). Synagogues were essential to Jewish communal life and reinforced the centrality of Scripture in their culture.

In synagogues, Jewish boys learned not only to read scripture but to interpret and debate its meanings, which was a core aspect of Jewish education. This practice of debate and interpretation is seen in Luke 2:46-47, where Jesus, as a young boy, sits among the teachers in the temple, "listening to them and asking them questions." His deep understanding and insightful questions astonished His listeners, foreshadowing His later role as a teacher who challenged and expanded their understanding of the Law.

- **1c. Jesus' Approach to Education: A Radical Departure**

Jesus grew up within this educational tradition but chose a remarkably different path in His teaching method. Rather than seeking out the educated elite, Jesus called fishermen, tax collectors, and everyday people to be His disciples (Matthew 4:18-22, Mark 2:14). This choice was radical in a society where formal education was highly respected and often limited to those of higher social status. Jesus' disciples, like Peter and John, were described as "unschooled, ordinary men" (Acts 4:13), yet they were chosen to carry forward His teachings.

By choosing such individuals, Jesus demonstrated that understanding and applying God's truth was not confined to the educated or privileged. His method contrasted with the scholarly approach of the rabbis, who required rigorous adherence to tradition and often debated nuances of the Law. Instead, Jesus emphasized transformation of the heart and mind. In Matthew 11:25, Jesus thanks His Father for hiding "these things from the wise and learned" and revealing them "to little children." His approach welcomed anyone willing to learn and follow Him, regardless of background.

- **1d. Scripture References to the Importance of Education and Discipleship**

Throughout the Bible, education and teaching hold significant value, and learning the ways of God is encouraged. In Deuteronomy 6:6-7, God commands the Israelites to impress His commandments on their children: "Talk about them when you sit at home and when you walk along the road, when you lie down and when you get up." This emphasizes a continuous, integrated approach to teaching and learning, where the knowledge of God's word is embedded in daily life. Jesus embodied this method by teaching His disciples during their journeys, at meals, and in all circumstances.

In Proverbs, we find another emphasis on wisdom and instruction. Proverbs 4:13 states, "Hold on to instruction, do not let it go; guard it well, for it is your life." This wisdom tradition underpinned the Jewish focus on the Law as a guide to life. Jesus respected this tradition, but He expanded it by revealing the heart of the Law—love for God and neighbor (Matthew 22:37-40). His teachings focused on the inner transformation that enables obedience, rather than mere adherence to rules.

In Matthew 28:19-20, Jesus gives His Great Commission to His disciples, telling them to "go and make disciples of all nations... teaching them to obey everything I have commanded you." This command underscores the importance Jesus placed on teaching and discipleship, not just as a transfer of knowledge, but as a calling to transform lives through living and learning in relationship with Him.

- **1e. A Model of Relational and Inclusive Discipleship**

While Jesus respected the value of Jewish educational traditions, He redefined the concept of discipleship. He did not establish schools or require prior learning; instead, He called people into a personal journey of faith and transformation. His disciples were expected to follow Him, learn from His example, and internalize His teachings. This approach made discipleship accessible to everyone, regardless of social status or educational background.

In choosing this method, Jesus demonstrated that true understanding comes not from rote learning but from a relationship with the Teacher Himself. His disciples learned by walking with Him, observing His actions, and absorbing His character. This immersive, relational model of discipleship became the foundation for a movement that would change the world.

Chapter 2
Choosing the Twelve - The Heart of Jesus' Method

Jesus' choice of disciples was unconventional and revolutionary for His time. In first-century Judea, religious leaders often sought disciples from among the highly educated or the socially elite, preferring students who could uphold their reputation and reinforce the authority of their teachings. Rabbis traditionally chose students who had shown exceptional knowledge and adherence to the Law, often individuals from prominent or educated families who had studied the Torah from an early age. However, Jesus took a different path, choosing ordinary people to accompany Him on His mission, thus redefining what it meant to be a disciple and opening the doors of discipleship to everyone.

- 2a. Historical Context: The Traditional Choice of Disciples

In Jewish tradition, rabbis would select disciples who were well-versed in the Scriptures and could demonstrate potential to carry on their teachings. This practice was deeply rooted in the Pharisaic and Sadducean schools of thought, where strict adherence to the Law was emphasized. A potential disciple would need to be someone who showed aptitude in study and debate, as religious leaders often engaged in lengthy discussions regarding interpretations of the Law.

These discipleship relationships were formal and hierarchical. Students were expected to commit entirely to their rabbi's teachings, often following him closely and attempting to emulate him in every aspect of life. The rabbi-disciple relationship was marked by a distance between the master and his student; disciples learned primarily through listening, observing, and repeating what the rabbi taught. This traditional approach kept religious education within the reach of the privileged few, limiting access to those who could dedicate years to strict study under a rabbi's authority.

- 2b. Jesus' Radical Choice of Disciples

Jesus' choice to call fishermen, tax collectors, and other ordinary men to be His disciples was extraordinary in several ways. In Matthew 4:18-22, Jesus calls Simon Peter and his brother Andrew while they are casting their nets. He then calls James and John, sons of Zebedee, who are also fishermen. None of these men had the qualifications expected of disciples in their society—they were neither educated in religious law nor respected in scholarly circles. Choosing them was, in essence, a challenge to the established religious norms.

One of the most notable examples of Jesus' unconventional choices is His call to Matthew, a tax collector (Matthew 9:9). Tax collectors were despised in Jewish society; they were seen as collaborators with the Roman occupiers and were often associated with corruption. By inviting Matthew to follow Him, Jesus displayed a radical inclusiveness, valuing the heart and willingness of an individual over societal reputation or past actions. His choice of Matthew illustrated His message that He came "not to call the righteous, but sinners" (Mark 2:17), opening the way for all people to come to God regardless of their past.

Jesus' selection of the Twelve—ordinary, flawed individuals—was intentional. It demonstrated His commitment to transforming lives from within and highlighted His power to redeem and empower people for His purpose. In Acts 4:13, Peter and John, two of Jesus' earliest disciples, are described as "unschooled, ordinary men," yet the people around them recognized "that they had been with Jesus." This statement underscores the transformative impact of being chosen by Jesus and trained under His guidance.

- 2c. The Call to Follow: A Personal Invitation

Unlike the typical rabbi-disciple relationship, Jesus' invitation to follow Him was a call to personal relationship and transformation. He did not ask His disciples to study or adhere to a formal set of principles but invited them to "come and see" (John 1:39) and to learn from His example. This approach allowed the disciples to observe Jesus' interactions, His compassion, His responses to opposition, and His prayer life. It was a deeply relational and experiential form of learning, one that called for the disciples' full engagement and commitment.

When Jesus called Simon Peter and Andrew, He said, "Follow me, and I will make you fishers of men" (Matthew 4:19). This invitation not only redefined their vocation but also conveyed Jesus' vision for their lives. The act of following Jesus meant surrendering their own goals and adopting a new identity as His disciples. This radical invitation required trust, as the disciples left their livelihoods, families, and familiar surroundings to journey with Jesus.

In Luke 9:23, Jesus makes the terms of discipleship clear: "Whoever wants to be my disciple must deny themselves and take up their cross daily and follow me." This call was not for the faint-hearted; it required a willingness to set aside one's personal ambitions, pride, and even one's life. Jesus' discipleship was a journey of self-denial, humility, and service—qualities that were in stark contrast to the status-driven culture of the time.

- 2d. The Impact of Jesus' Choice: A Model for Relational Discipleship

By choosing disciples who were ordinary people, Jesus modeled a form of discipleship that was relational, inclusive, and deeply personal. His disciples were not just students; they became His friends and confidants. In John 15:15, Jesus says, "I no longer call you servants, because a servant does not know his master's business. Instead, I have called you friends, for everything that I learned from my Father I have made known to you." This shift from servanthood to friendship marked a new kind of relationship between teacher and disciple—one based on mutual love and shared purpose.

Through this relational approach, Jesus imparted His values and teachings in a way that transformed the lives of His disciples. His daily presence with them allowed them to see His compassion for the marginalized, His integrity, His patience, and His faithfulness in every situation. They were not only learning doctrines or principles but were absorbing the very nature and character of their Teacher. In this way, Jesus' discipleship was as much about character formation as it was about imparting knowledge.

Jesus' selection of the Twelve also set a precedent for the mission of the church. In Matthew 28:19-20, after His resurrection, Jesus commissions His disciples to "go and make disciples of all nations." Just as Jesus had called them, He now sends them to invite others into this same life of discipleship. The early church followed this relational model, as seen in the close-knit communities described in Acts, where believers shared their lives, prayed together, and encouraged one another in faith (Acts 2:42-47).

- **2e. Biblical References on God's Choice of the Humble and Ordinary**

Jesus' choice of ordinary disciples reflects a biblical theme: God often chooses the humble and unlikely to accomplish His purposes. In 1

Samuel 16:7, when Samuel is sent to anoint a new king, God reminds him, "The Lord does not look at the things people look at. People look at the outward appearance, but the Lord looks at the heart." This principle is seen in Jesus' choices, as He looks beyond social standing or qualifications to the potential within each individual.

Similarly, Paul writes in 1 Corinthians 1:26-29, "God chose the foolish things of the world to shame the wise; God chose the weak things of the world to shame the strong." Jesus' disciples embodied this principle, as their lives and testimonies demonstrated the transformative power of God. Though they were "unschooled and ordinary" by worldly standards, they became foundational figures in the spread of the Gospel and the establishment of the early church.

- **2f. Jesus' Approach to Discipleship as a Model of Empowerment**

Jesus' choice of disciples illustrates a key aspect of His teaching method: empowerment. By choosing those whom society overlooked, He showed that the ability to fulfill God's purposes comes not from human qualifications but from divine calling and guidance. Jesus empowered His disciples by inviting them to share in His life, teaching them not only through words but through example and presence.

Through His relational approach, Jesus gave His disciples more than knowledge; He gave them a vision for their lives and a mission that would outlast His earthly ministry. They became "fishers of men," a new vocation that reached beyond personal goals and into the realm of Kingdom work. This model of empowerment continues to inspire Christians today, reminding us that Jesus calls each of us not based on our qualifications but on our willingness to follow, learn, and grow in relationship with Him.

Chapter 3
Learning by Example - The Power of Modeling

One of the most powerful aspects of Jesus' teaching method was His emphasis on *modeling*. Unlike traditional teachers who relied primarily on instruction, Jesus used His life as a living lesson, demonstrating the principles He taught. This approach allowed His disciples to observe His actions, witness His interactions, and experience His love, compassion, and faith firsthand. In many ways, Jesus' life was His curriculum; He didn't just teach concepts—He embodied them. By modeling His teachings, Jesus provided His disciples with a tangible, lasting example of how to live, love, and serve.

- 3a. The Historical and Cultural Significance of Modeling in Jewish Education

In ancient Jewish culture, modeling was an integral part of learning. Jewish rabbis, particularly those in the Pharisaic tradition, valued the practice of discipleship not just as a means to gain knowledge but as a pathway to becoming more like the teacher. Discipleship often involved living closely with a rabbi, observing his conduct, and emulating his lifestyle. This idea of imitation was especially relevant in the Jewish understanding of wisdom, where true learning was seen as transforming one's character and behavior, not merely acquiring information.

The Hebrew concept of *halakhah*, which means "the way" or "the path," encompassed this principle. To walk in "the way" of the rabbi was to adopt his beliefs, actions, and attitudes as a guide for one's own life. Jesus embodied this tradition in an even deeper way, inviting His disciples not only to learn His teachings but to live them out as He did. Unlike many rabbis of His time, Jesus did not only instruct His disciples in the synagogue or formal settings; He allowed them to walk with Him, observe Him, and share in His daily life.

- **3b. Jesus' Approach to Modeling and the Transformative Power of Example**

Jesus' teaching through example went beyond mere instruction. He intentionally demonstrated the virtues and principles of the Kingdom of God in every aspect of His life. His disciples saw Him interact with people from all walks of life—the poor, the sick, the outcasts, and the wealthy. Jesus' compassion, kindness, patience, and wisdom became visible to His followers, providing a practical model for how they, too, were to live and serve.

For instance, when Jesus healed the leper (Mark 1:40-42), He not only healed but touched the man, an act that was considered culturally taboo, as lepers were seen as unclean. By touching the leper, Jesus showed His disciples that compassion and love transcended societal boundaries. He demonstrated that God's love was inclusive, even toward those whom society rejected. This act was not merely a lesson in kindness; it was a radical model of how the disciples were to treat others, challenging their cultural preconceptions and teaching them to see people through God's eyes.

Another powerful example of Jesus' modeling is seen when He washed His disciples' feet. In John 13:1-17, Jesus takes on the role of a servant, washing His disciples' feet—an act typically reserved for the lowest servant in a household. After completing this humble act, He says to them, "I have set you an example that you should do as I have done for you" (John 13:15). This example of servant leadership was revolutionary, as it directly challenged the societal norms of authority and power. Jesus taught His disciples that true greatness in His Kingdom was marked by humility and service to others, a principle they would carry into their own ministries.

- 3c. The Influence of Jesus' Modeling on the Disciples' Character Development

By consistently modeling His teachings, Jesus provided His disciples with more than information—He offered them a vision of what they could become. His example influenced their character, transforming them from impulsive, self-centered individuals into compassionate, courageous leaders. This transformation is most evident in Peter, who, at the beginning of his journey, often acted impulsively and out of fear. However, after witnessing Jesus' patience, humility, and boldness, Peter himself became a bold proclaimer of the Gospel, even in the face of persecution (Acts 2:14-41).

Another example of character transformation can be seen in John, who went from being known as one of the "sons of thunder" (Mark 3:17), known for his fiery temperament, to being remembered as the "apostle of love." John's letters, especially 1 John, are filled with themes of love, compassion, and unity—principles he learned by observing Jesus' life. Jesus' modeling provided John with a new understanding of love that transcended his initial disposition, reshaping his character in alignment with Christ's values.

In Galatians 4:19, Paul later describes the goal of discipleship as forming Christ within each believer: "My dear children, for whom I am again in the pains of childbirth until Christ is formed in you." This concept reflects the influence of Jesus' modeling, where the ultimate purpose of discipleship is to shape the character of the disciple in the likeness of Christ. Jesus' example became the foundation for this transformation, demonstrating that true discipleship is not merely about following rules but about embodying the heart and character of the Teacher.

- **3d. Biblical References Illustrating the Power of Example**

The power of example is a consistent theme throughout Scripture, emphasizing the idea that actions often speak louder than words. In 1 Corinthians 11:1, Paul echoes this principle, urging believers to "follow my example, as I follow the example of Christ." This statement highlights that discipleship is about imitating Christlike behavior, which in turn becomes a model for others. The effectiveness of Jesus' method lies in the way His life serves as a template for His followers, inspiring them to live out their faith in tangible, practical ways.

The apostle Peter also emphasizes the power of example in 1 Peter 2:21, saying, "To this you were called, because Christ suffered for you, leaving you an example, that you should follow in his steps." This passage acknowledges that following Jesus' example is not always easy; it requires sacrifice, patience, and often, enduring hardship. Yet, it is through this process that believers grow in likeness to Christ, embodying His love, humility, and resilience.

In the Old Testament, the concept of modeling is seen in God's call to His people to be a "light to the nations" (Isaiah 42:6). Israel was called to live in a way that reflected God's righteousness and compassion so that other nations might see God's character through them. This theme of being an example continued in Jesus' ministry, where His disciples were called to be "the light of the world" (Matthew 5:14-16), reflecting God's love and truth in their actions and character.

- 3e. The Lasting Impact of Jesus' Example on His Disciples and the Early Church

Jesus' emphasis on modeling left a lasting impact on His disciples and became foundational to the early church. After Jesus' ascension, the disciples carried forward His teachings and, more importantly, His example. They became known not just for their words but for their way of life, a life marked by humility, compassion, and sacrificial love. In Acts 2:42-47, we see a picture of the early church that mirrors the example Jesus set: believers shared everything in common, cared for one another's needs, and lived in unity.

This sense of communal life and self-sacrifice, inspired by Jesus' example, was one of the defining features of the early Christian community. Their actions set them apart, drawing others to Christ not only through preaching but through the witness of their lives. As Tertullian, an early church father, famously observed, "See how they love one another!" This legacy of modeling has continued through generations, with each believer called to reflect the character of Christ as a testimony to the world.

- 3f. Modeling as the Heart of True Discipleship

Jesus' use of modeling as a teaching method highlights an essential truth about discipleship: transformation happens not only through what is taught but through what is lived. By living among His disciples and showing them how to love, serve, and sacrifice, Jesus imparted lessons that went far deeper than words. His life was a living example, one that challenged cultural norms, redefined greatness, and revealed God's heart.

Jesus' example continues to serve as a guide for Christians today, reminding us that our actions, attitudes, and relationships are as powerful a witness as our words. In following His example, we are called to embody His love, compassion, and humility, allowing His life to shine through ours. This legacy of modeling is the heart of true discipleship, a journey not only of learning but of becoming—transformed into the image of the Master Teacher.

Chapter 4
Teaching in Parables - Simplifying the Profound

One of the most distinctive features of Jesus' teaching method was His use of parables—simple, relatable stories that conveyed profound spiritual truths. Parables were more than illustrations; they were a way of engaging listeners, inviting them to see deeper meanings beneath the surface. For Jesus, parables were a tool to reveal the mysteries of the Kingdom of God, using everyday images and scenarios familiar to His audience, making spiritual truths accessible to everyone.

Parables had a transformative power. They encouraged listeners to explore, question, and reflect, creating a personal journey toward understanding. As we examine Jesus' use of parables, we see how this method not only simplified profound concepts but also provided insight into the nature of God, the Kingdom, and the path of discipleship.

- **4a. Historical and Cultural Background of Parables in Jewish Teaching**

Parables were a common form of teaching in Jewish tradition. Rabbis often used stories, allegories, and metaphors to explain complex theological ideas, and the Jewish people were familiar with this style. The Hebrew Scriptures include examples of parable-like teachings, such as Nathan's story to King David about the rich man and the poor man's lamb (2 Samuel 12:1-7), which used metaphor to bring conviction and reveal deeper truths.

In ancient Jewish culture, storytelling was valued not only as a way to preserve history but also as a means of conveying moral lessons and wisdom. Proverbs, for example, are filled with vivid imagery and practical insights about life, character, and morality. This context provided a foundation for Jesus' audience to understand and appreciate parables as a form of teaching that invited reflection and self-examination. However, unlike the typical parables of the time, Jesus' stories often had an unexpected twist or deeper meaning that challenged conventional thinking, inviting His listeners into a new understanding of God and His Kingdom.

- **4b. The Purpose of Parables in Jesus' Ministry**

When asked by His disciples why He taught in parables, Jesus explained, "The knowledge of the secrets of the kingdom of heaven has been given to you, but not to them... This is why I speak to them in parables" (Matthew 13:11,13). Parables served as both revelation and concealment—they revealed truths to those open to receiving them, while remaining hidden to those who were not prepared to understand.

This approach reflects Jesus' intention to engage His listeners in a process of seeking and discovery. He knew that a direct, literal explanation might not penetrate the hearts of those who were resistant to change or unwilling to embrace His teachings. By using parables, Jesus encouraged His audience to think deeply, ask questions, and grapple with the meaning of His words. The parables functioned as a mirror, reflecting back the listener's own spiritual state and inviting them to engage with the message on a personal level.

- **4c. Key Parables and Their Significance**

Several of Jesus' most well-known parables offer valuable insights into the nature of the Kingdom of God, human character, and the path of discipleship. Let's examine a few of these parables and the profound truths they reveal.

The Parable of the Sower (Matthew 13:3-9, 18-23): In this parable, Jesus describes a farmer who sows seeds on different types of soil, each representing a different response to God's word. Some seeds fall on the path and are eaten by birds, others fall on rocky soil and wither, some fall among thorns and are choked, and others fall on good soil and produce a crop. This parable illustrates the various ways people receive God's message, highlighting that spiritual growth depends on the condition of one's heart. Jesus uses the metaphor of soil to show that openness, receptivity, and perseverance are essential for His teachings to take root in a person's life.

The Parable of the Good Samaritan (Luke 10:25-37): In this story, Jesus challenges social norms and expectations by depicting a Samaritan—someone despised by Jewish society—as the hero who shows mercy to a wounded traveler, while a priest and a Levite pass by without helping. This parable illustrates the command to "love your neighbor as yourself," expanding the definition of "neighbor" beyond cultural and ethnic boundaries. The story conveys that true discipleship is marked by compassion and action, regardless of social divisions.

The Parable of the Prodigal Son (Luke 15:11-32): This parable is one of Jesus' most famous and powerful teachings. In it, a son demands his inheritance, squanders it, and eventually returns home, expecting rejection but instead receiving his father's forgiveness and love. This story reveals the heart of God as a loving Father who welcomes sinners with open arms. The parable conveys profound truths about repentance, grace, and the boundless love of God, challenging listeners to reflect on their own understanding of forgiveness and mercy.

Each of these parables not only conveyed a specific lesson but also challenged the listeners to reconsider their understanding of God, themselves, and others. Through stories, Jesus communicated truths that could not easily be expressed in straightforward terms, allowing listeners to see their own lives and actions in light of the Kingdom.

- **4d. The Role of Mystery and Revelation in Parables**

Jesus' parables were intentionally layered with mystery, offering insights that went beyond surface understanding. This use of mystery served a dual purpose. First, it protected the message from those who were hostile or unready to accept it. Second, it invited genuine seekers to pursue deeper understanding. As Jesus said, "He who has ears to hear, let him hear" (Mark 4:9). This statement invited those who were spiritually attentive to engage with the message and seek its deeper meaning.

In Matthew 13:34-35, it is written, "Jesus spoke all these things to the crowd in parables... So was fulfilled what was spoken through the prophet: 'I will open my mouth in parables, I will utter things hidden since the creation of the world.'" By using parables, Jesus was fulfilling the prophetic tradition of revealing God's wisdom in unexpected ways. Parables became a means of revealing eternal truths that had been hidden throughout history, drawing back the veil for those who were ready to understand.

The disciples themselves often needed further explanation of the parables. For example, in Mark 4:10-12, Jesus provides His disciples with a more in-depth interpretation of the Parable of the Sower, explaining that the different soils represent different responses to the

Word of God. This inner circle of disciples received greater insight, preparing them to later share these truths with others.

- **4e. Parables as Invitations to Transformation**

Jesus' parables were not merely stories for entertainment or intellectual engagement; they were invitations to transformation. Each parable contains a call to action, encouraging the listener to respond in faith, repentance, or a deeper commitment to the Kingdom of God. Parables were designed to move listeners from passive observation to active decision-making.

For instance, the Parable of the Wise and Foolish Builders (Matthew 7:24-27) presents a choice: to build one's life on the solid foundation of Jesus' teachings or on the shifting sands of worldly values. Jesus concludes this parable by saying, "Therefore everyone who hears these words of mine and puts them into practice is like a wise man who built his house on the rock." This parable is a call to not only hear but to apply His teachings, emphasizing that true discipleship involves a commitment to living out the truths He taught.

In the Parable of the Ten Virgins (Matthew 25:1-13), Jesus emphasizes the importance of readiness for His return, urging His followers to live lives marked by vigilance and faithfulness. This story is a powerful reminder that the Kingdom of God requires preparation, and that disciples must be prepared to meet the King whenever He returns. The parable invites listeners to reflect on their own spiritual readiness and commitment to the path of discipleship.

- ### 4f. The Power of Parables in Modern Discipleship

The timeless nature of Jesus' parables allows them to resonate across generations and cultures. Even today, parables remain effective tools for teaching, as they invite readers to engage their hearts and minds, prompting self-reflection and personal application. The simplicity and depth of parables provide access to the truths of God's Kingdom in a way that is relevant to both the scholarly and the uneducated, the young and the old.

In modern discipleship, parables continue to inspire believers to seek a deeper understanding of their faith, challenging them to live out the principles of love, forgiveness, humility, and faithfulness. They encourage disciples to look beyond the literal and to search for the deeper meanings in life, relationships, and faith.

The legacy of Jesus' parables serves as a model for Christian educators, leaders, and believers, encouraging them to communicate complex truths in ways that are accessible and relatable. The parables remind us that the Kingdom of God is near, accessible, and relevant, inviting all who are willing to come, listen, and discover its mysteries.

- ### 4g. The Lasting Impact of Jesus' Parables

Through parables, Jesus simplified profound spiritual truths, making them accessible to all and inviting each listener to a journey of discovery. His stories, drawn from the ordinary, revealed the extraordinary nature of God's love, mercy, and justice. Parables continue to invite believers into a deeper relationship with God, as they compel us to consider, reflect, and transform.

In the end, Jesus' parables are a testament to His wisdom and His deep understanding of the human heart.

Chapter 5
Empowering and Sending Out - Practical Application

A vital aspect of Jesus' discipleship method was His focus on empowering His disciples and sending them out to put their learning into practice. Jesus' teachings were never intended to be theoretical or confined to intellectual understanding alone; rather, they were to be lived out. To ensure that His disciples truly grasped the essence of His message, Jesus equipped them with authority, purpose, and the confidence to engage in hands-on ministry. This approach emphasized the importance of learning through experience, allowing the disciples to internalize His teachings, face real challenges, and deepen their dependence on God.

- 5a. Historical Context: Learning Through Apprenticeship

In first-century Jewish culture, apprenticeship was a common method for learning a trade or skill. Young men who aspired to become craftsmen, carpenters, or fishermen learned by working alongside an experienced master. This process allowed apprentices to observe, imitate, and eventually take on responsibilities of their own under the guidance of their mentor. Similarly, religious discipleship involved close association with a rabbi or teacher, learning not only by listening but by doing.

Jesus adapted this model into a powerful method of spiritual training. His disciples did not just learn by sitting in synagogues or listening to lectures; they learned by following Him on His journeys, observing His miracles, and eventually participating in His work. This experiential approach gave them a sense of purpose and ownership over the mission they would one day carry forward independently.

- 5b. The Empowerment of the Twelve and Seventy-Two

One of the defining moments of Jesus' discipleship method was His decision to give the Twelve apostles authority and send them out to minister. In Matthew 10:1, it states, "Jesus called His twelve disciples to Him and gave them authority to drive out impure spirits and to heal every disease and sickness." This was a remarkable act of empowerment, as Jesus entrusted His disciples with the very authority that He had demonstrated through His miracles.

In the following verses, Jesus provides them with specific instructions, saying, "As you go, proclaim this message: 'The kingdom of heaven has come near.' Heal the sick, raise the dead, cleanse those who have leprosy, drive out demons. Freely you have received; freely give" (Matthew 10:7-8). Jesus not only gave them authority but also a clear mission: to proclaim the Kingdom and demonstrate its power through acts of compassion and healing.

Later, in Luke 10:1-20, Jesus expands this mission by sending out seventy-two disciples in pairs. This broader group was also empowered to heal and proclaim the Kingdom. The disciples returned with joy, saying, "Lord, even the demons submit to us in Your name" (Luke 10:17). This experience not only strengthened their faith but also helped them to understand the power and authority that came through their connection to Jesus.

By sending out His disciples, Jesus demonstrated that His mission was not something to be guarded or monopolized but something to be shared. He entrusted His followers with real responsibility, allowing them to grow in faith and skill as they engaged in hands-on ministry.

- **5c. Facing Challenges and Developing Resilience**

Jesus knew that practical ministry would expose His disciples to rejection, opposition, and hardship. When sending them out, He prepared them for the realities of ministry by warning them of the challenges they would face. In Matthew 10:16, Jesus says, "I am sending you out like sheep among wolves. Therefore be as shrewd as snakes and as innocent as doves." This statement highlighted the need for wisdom, discernment, and perseverance.

The disciples encountered both acceptance and rejection, and each experience helped shape their character. In Luke 9:5, Jesus instructs them, "If people do not welcome you, leave their town and shake the dust off your feet as a testimony against them." This instruction taught the disciples to remain focused on their mission without being discouraged by opposition.

Jesus' empowerment of His disciples included teaching them to rely on God's provision. He instructed them not to take money, extra clothes, or provisions, emphasizing that they should depend on the hospitality of those who would receive them (Luke 10:4-7). This lesson of reliance on God was a crucial part of their training, reinforcing the understanding that their success was not based on their own resources or abilities but on God's provision and guidance.

Through these experiences, the disciples developed resilience, adaptability, and a deeper trust in God. By allowing them to face real-world challenges, Jesus prepared them to become leaders who could endure hardships and stay faithful to their calling.

- 5d. Biblical Examples of Empowerment in Jesus' Ministry

Jesus' empowerment of His disciples was consistent with the biblical principle of God calling ordinary people to extraordinary tasks. In the Old Testament, God often chose individuals who felt unqualified for the work He set before them, like Moses, who was reluctant to speak to Pharaoh (Exodus 4:10-12), or Gideon, who doubted his own strength (Judges 6:15-16). Jesus' choice of fishermen, tax collectors, and other ordinary men to carry His message aligns with this theme, showing that God equips those He calls.

The disciples' empowerment was also a foreshadowing of the Great Commission, in which Jesus would later send them to make disciples of all nations (Matthew 28:19-20). Before His ascension, Jesus assures them, "You will receive power when the Holy Spirit comes on you; and you will be my witnesses in Jerusalem, and in all Judea and Samaria, and to the ends of the earth" (Acts 1:8). The practical experience they gained while Jesus was with them prepared them to carry forward the mission once they received the Holy Spirit's power.

- **5e. Practical Application and the Role of the Holy Spirit**

Jesus' method of empowerment included not only granting authority but also instilling a dependency on the Holy Spirit. In John 14:26, Jesus promises His disciples that the Holy Spirit will "teach you all things and will remind you of everything I have said to you." He emphasized that their success in ministry would come not from their own strength but from the guidance and empowerment of the Spirit.

The Book of Acts provides numerous examples of the disciples operating under the power of the Holy Spirit. Peter, once timid and fearful, becomes a bold preacher on the day of Pentecost, proclaiming the message of Christ to a large crowd (Acts 2:14-41). Similarly,

Stephen, one of the early deacons, performs great signs and wonders among the people and courageously testifies to the truth of the Gospel, even to the point of martyrdom (Acts 6:8-10, Acts 7:54-60). The empowerment Jesus provided, combined with the guidance of the Holy Spirit, enabled the disciples to accomplish extraordinary things for the Kingdom of God.

This reliance on the Holy Spirit continues to be foundational for Christian ministry today. Jesus' example reminds us that true empowerment in ministry involves surrendering our own agendas, seeking God's will, and relying on the Spirit's guidance.

- 5f. The Impact of Sending Out on the Disciples' Growth

The experience of being sent out to minister had a profound impact on the disciples' growth and faith. Through hands-on ministry, they learned about the challenges and joys of serving God's Kingdom. They developed confidence in the authority they had received, witnessing the power of God working through them. This confidence and experience became essential as they later faced greater challenges in building the early church.

The disciples also learned humility through these experiences. They encountered situations that reminded them of their need for God's power and presence. For instance, in Matthew 17:14-21, the disciples were unable to cast out a demon, prompting Jesus to remind them of the importance of faith and prayer. These moments of failure were as instructive as their successes, teaching them dependence on God rather than on their own abilities.

When Jesus finally commissioned His disciples to "go and make disciples of all nations" (Matthew 28:19-20), they were ready. They had already tasted both the joys and difficulties of ministry. They had learned to trust God, to rely on each other, and to stay faithful even in the face of opposition. Their experience of being sent out was not just preparation; it was the beginning of a lifelong mission that would change the world.

- **5g. The Call to Practical Application in Modern Discipleship**

Jesus' approach of sending His disciples to put His teachings into practice is a powerful model for modern discipleship. In today's church, believers are often taught about faith but may lack opportunities to actively practice it. Jesus' example encourages us to see discipleship not as mere learning but as a process that involves real-life application, where faith is exercised and tested.

Modern discipleship benefits greatly from hands-on ministry, where believers are given opportunities to serve, teach, lead, and make a difference. By participating in outreach, sharing their faith, or volunteering in various capacities, believers today can experience the growth and transformation that come from putting their faith into action. The early church thrived because it followed this model, engaging believers in active service and encouraging them to use their gifts for God's glory.

Jesus' method reminds us that true discipleship involves both learning and doing. It is in the doing—facing challenges, serving others, relying on God—that disciples grow in maturity, faith, and love.

- 5h. Empowering Disciples to Transform the World

Jesus' empowerment of His disciples through hands-on ministry was a cornerstone of His teaching method. By giving them authority, purpose, and the opportunity to put His teachings into practice, He prepared them for a mission that would continue long after His departure.

Chapter 6
The Role of Questions and Reflection

Throughout His ministry, Jesus used questions as a central part of His teaching method. He didn't always provide His disciples with straightforward answers; instead, He encouraged them to reflect, to examine themselves, and to consider their own beliefs and assumptions. Jesus' questions were intentional and thought-provoking, leading His followers to discover truths within themselves and to deepen their relationship with God.

In using questions, Jesus invited His disciples into an interactive learning experience. His questions were rarely rhetorical; they demanded a response, drawing His listeners into a dialogue that would challenge their minds and engage their hearts. This approach to teaching reflected the Jewish tradition of questioning and debate but added a transformative spiritual dimension that invited self-reflection and personal commitment.

- 6a. The Tradition of Questioning in Jewish Culture

In Jewish culture, questioning was a respected part of learning and dialogue. Rabbis often engaged in debate, using questions to clarify theological points, explore interpretations of the Law, and examine moral and ethical issues. In this context, a question was not a sign of ignorance but a starting point for deeper insight. Through questions, students were encouraged to search the Scriptures, consider multiple perspectives, and refine their understanding.

This tradition of questioning is seen throughout the Hebrew Scriptures. For example, in the book of Job, Job and his friends wrestle with questions about suffering, justice, and God's character. The Psalms also contain questions directed toward God, reflecting the psalmists' struggles and search for understanding. Jesus embraced this tradition but used questions in a way that went beyond intellectual inquiry, focusing on the heart and encouraging His disciples to look within.

- ## 6b. Jesus' Use of Questions in His Teaching

Jesus used questions to challenge His followers' assumptions, expose their doubts, and reveal deeper truths. His questions often addressed the heart of the matter, prompting self-examination and personal reflection. Here are a few examples that highlight the profound impact of Jesus' questioning approach:

"**Who do you say that I am?**" (Matthew 16:15): This question, directed at His disciples, went beyond theology and touched on personal conviction. When Peter responded, "You are the Messiah, the Son of the living God" (Matthew 16:16), he was making a personal declaration of faith. Jesus' question required His disciples to confront their own understanding of who He was, moving them from curiosity to commitment.

"**Why are you afraid, O you of little faith?**" (Matthew 8:26): When the disciples were frightened by a storm while crossing the Sea of Galilee, Jesus' question pointed to their underlying fear and lack of trust. His question was both a gentle rebuke and an invitation to faith. Through this question, Jesus encouraged them to examine the source of their fear and to recognize their need for deeper trust in Him.

"**What do you want Me to do for you?**" (Mark 10:51): Jesus asked this question to a blind man seeking healing. Rather than assuming what the man wanted, Jesus invited him to articulate his desire. This question emphasized the importance of approaching God with faith and clarity, encouraging individuals to voice their needs and express their dependence on God's grace.

Each of these questions served a purpose beyond simply gathering information. Jesus' questions were designed to probe the heart, uncover hidden fears, and invite the listener to step into a deeper relationship with God. They fostered a space for genuine transformation by leading people to confront their own motives, beliefs, and desires.

- 6c. The Power of Questions in Fostering Self-Reflection and Growth

Jesus' questioning approach allowed His disciples to think critically, consider their own spiritual journey, and examine their values. Instead of simply telling them what to believe, Jesus asked questions that made them consider why they believed and acted the way they did. This technique encouraged a personal engagement with faith, fostering maturity and independence in their understanding.

By asking questions, Jesus also modeled humility. He wasn't forceful or authoritarian; He didn't dictate His disciples' responses. Instead, He allowed them to come to their conclusions through guided reflection. This created a safe environment for learning, where the disciples could ask questions, admit their doubts, and grow in their understanding.

In Luke 10:25-37, Jesus uses a question to initiate the Parable of the Good Samaritan. A lawyer asks, "What must I do to inherit eternal life?" Jesus responds by asking, "What is written in the Law? How do you read it?" This interaction not only acknowledges the lawyer's question but empowers him to interpret and understand the Law himself. When the lawyer further asks, "Who is my neighbor?" Jesus tells the parable, indirectly answering the question and challenging him to rethink the concept of neighborly love. Jesus' questions were an invitation for the lawyer—and for His disciples—to look beyond legal definitions and understand the essence of compassion and mercy.

- **6d. Jesus' Questions as a Means of Revelation**

Jesus often used questions to reveal spiritual truths in ways that simple statements might not. His questions served as a mirror, allowing individuals to see their own hearts and beliefs more clearly. In John 6, after Jesus had taught some challenging truths, many of His followers left Him. He turned to the Twelve and asked, "Do you also want to go away?" (John 6:67). This question revealed the depth of commitment among the disciples, prompting Peter to respond, "Lord, to whom shall we go? You have the words of eternal life" (John 6:68).

This question forced the disciples to confront their loyalty and commitment, highlighting the transformative nature of Jesus' teachings. Rather than pressuring them to stay, Jesus gave them the freedom to choose, revealing who truly understood His message and was willing to follow Him, even when it was difficult.

In Matthew 20:32, Jesus encounters two blind men who cry out to Him. He asks, "What do you want me to do for you?" This question may seem unnecessary, as it would be obvious that they wanted healing, but Jesus uses it to invite them to articulate their faith and need. Their response, "Lord, we want our sight," demonstrates their belief in His power and sets the stage for their healing.

- ### 6e. The Role of Questions in the Disciples' Spiritual Growth

The process of answering Jesus' questions encouraged the disciples to consider their values, beliefs, and identity. These questions were an essential part of their spiritual growth, as they taught the disciples to think deeply and to develop a faith that was personal and self-aware. By answering questions like "Who do you say that I am?" they moved from being observers to active participants in their own faith journey.

In John 21:15-17, after His resurrection, Jesus uses a series of questions to restore Peter, who had denied Him three times. He asks, "Simon son of John, do you love me?" Jesus repeats this question three times, mirroring Peter's three denials. Each repetition invites Peter to reaffirm his love and commitment, helping him to move past his failure and step into his role as a leader. Jesus' questioning here is not punitive but redemptive, guiding Peter toward forgiveness, restoration, and a renewed sense of purpose.

Through these encounters, the disciples learned that questions were not a sign of weakness or doubt; rather, they were an invitation to go deeper. Jesus' use of questions taught them that faith was not about having all the answers but about being open to growth, reflection, and discovery.

- ### 6f. The Impact of Jesus' Questioning Method on the Early Church

The questioning approach that Jesus used had a lasting impact on His disciples and the early church. As the disciples began to teach and lead others, they continued to use questions to foster growth, self-examination, and engagement with the Gospel. This is evident in the letters of Paul, who often used rhetorical questions to provoke thought and challenge his readers.

For example, in Romans 8:31, Paul asks, "If God is for us, who can be against us?" This question invites believers to reflect on the security of their relationship with God, reinforcing their confidence and trust. In Galatians 3:1, Paul questions the Galatian church, "Who has bewitched you?" as a way of challenging them to examine the influences that were leading them away from the truth. Paul's use of questions reflects the influence of Jesus' teaching style, emphasizing that true faith is an active, reflective process.

The early church leaders understood that discipleship involved not only teaching doctrine but encouraging believers to engage deeply with their faith. This legacy of questioning has continued through centuries, emphasizing that the journey of faith is marked by ongoing reflection and a willingness to ask—and wrestle with—life's most important questions.

- 6g. Application of Jesus' Questioning Method in Modern Discipleship

In modern discipleship, the use of questions remains an essential tool for growth and self-examination. Jesus' example encourages mentors, pastors, and teachers to foster environments where questions are welcomed and encouraged. By inviting disciples to reflect, mentors can help them develop a deeper, more personal faith that is resilient and adaptable to life's challenges.

For today's believers, engaging with questions about faith, purpose, and personal values allows them to move beyond surface-level understanding and to embrace a faith that is rooted in self-awareness and genuine conviction. Jesus' questioning method teaches us that asking questions is not only acceptable but essential to spiritual maturity. It fosters humility, openness, and a willingness to grow, helping disciples cultivate a faith that is both intellectually and spiritually robust.

Whether through personal reflection, small group discussions, or one-on-one mentoring, the use of questions can lead to profound insights and spiritual transformation. By following Jesus' example, modern disciples

Chapter 7
The Final Lessons - Preparation for Independence

As Jesus' earthly ministry approached its conclusion, He began to prepare His disciples for the time when they would carry on His mission without His physical presence. These final lessons were among the most profound and essential teachings Jesus imparted, serving as a guide for His disciples to continue His work in a challenging world. He knew that they would face obstacles, persecution, and the responsibility of spreading His message across the world. To equip them for this mission, Jesus focused on lessons in humility, servant leadership, faith, resilience, and the power of the Holy Spirit. These parting teachings would lay the foundation for the early church and set a standard for Christian discipleship that remains relevant today.

- **7a. The Lesson of Servant Leadership**

One of the most memorable lessons Jesus taught His disciples in His final days was the principle of servant leadership. In John 13, on the night before His crucifixion, Jesus performed an act that shocked His disciples: He washed their feet. Foot washing was a task reserved for the lowest of servants, yet Jesus, their teacher and Lord, took on this role to demonstrate humility and service.

After washing their feet, Jesus told them, "Now that I, your Lord and Teacher, have washed your feet, you also should wash one another's feet. I have set you an example that you should do as I have done for you" (John 13:14-15). Through this act, Jesus redefined leadership, showing that true greatness in God's Kingdom was marked by humility and service to others. The disciples would carry this lesson into their ministry, modeling servant leadership as they established and led the early church.

This teaching was revolutionary, as it contrasted sharply with the cultural expectations of power and authority. By washing their feet, Jesus illustrated that His disciples were to lead through love and humility, putting others before themselves. This lesson of servant leadership became foundational for the disciples, who would later embody this principle in their relationships and their work. It was a reminder that their mission was not about seeking status or power but about serving others with a heart of compassion.

- **7b. Faith and Resilience in the Face of Persecution**

As Jesus prepared His disciples for their mission, He made it clear that following Him would not be easy. He warned them that they would face persecution and rejection, just as He had. In John 15:18-20, Jesus says, "If the world hates you, keep in mind that it hated me first… If they persecuted me, they will persecute you also." These words were meant to prepare the disciples for the difficulties they would encounter, helping them to develop resilience and unwavering faith.

Jesus did not sugarcoat the realities of discipleship. He told them plainly about the cost they would bear, yet He also encouraged them with words of hope. In John 16:33, He reassured them, saying, "In this world, you will have trouble. But take heart! I have overcome the world." This promise of victory over the world's trials gave the disciples the courage they would need to face opposition.

Through these lessons, Jesus showed His disciples that resilience and faith were crucial elements of their mission. Their calling would require courage and steadfastness, even in the face of adversity. This lesson remained with the disciples, who endured hardships, imprisonment, and martyrdom for the sake of the Gospel. Their willingness to suffer for their faith became a powerful testimony, inspiring others to follow Christ with the same resilience.

- 7c. The Promise of the Holy Spirit as a Helper and Guide

Jesus understood that His disciples could not accomplish their mission alone. In His final teachings, He assured them that they would not be left on their own; He would send them a Helper—the Holy Spirit. In John 14:16-17, Jesus promised, "I will ask the Father, and He will give you another advocate to help you and be with you forever—the Spirit of truth." The Holy Spirit would empower, guide, and comfort them, providing the wisdom and strength they needed to fulfill their calling.

In John 14:26, Jesus explained the role of the Holy Spirit further: "The Advocate, the Holy Spirit, whom the Father will send in my name, will teach you all things and will remind you of everything I have said to you." The Holy Spirit would be a teacher and a source of divine revelation, helping the disciples to recall and understand Jesus' teachings. This promise was fulfilled on the day of Pentecost, when the disciples were filled with the Holy Spirit and began to preach boldly (Acts 2:1-4).

The gift of the Holy Spirit was essential to the disciples' success in spreading the Gospel. Through the Spirit, they received wisdom, courage, and the ability to perform miracles in Jesus' name. The Holy Spirit transformed them from uncertain followers into bold leaders who would change the course of history. Jesus' promise of the Spirit's presence and guidance assured them that they would never be alone, even in the most difficult moments.

- **7d. The Great Commission: A Call to Make Disciples of All Nations**

Before ascending to heaven, Jesus gathered His disciples and gave them a final instruction, known as the Great Commission. In Matthew 28:18-20, He said, "All authority in heaven and on earth has been given to me. Therefore go and make disciples of all nations, baptizing them in the name of the Father and of the Son and of the Holy Spirit, and teaching them to obey everything I have commanded you. And surely I am with you always, to the very end of the age."

The Great Commission was both a command and a promise. Jesus empowered His disciples to carry His message to the ends of the earth, ensuring that they would have His presence with them as they went. This commission marked the beginning of the church's global mission, calling His followers to bring the message of salvation to all people.

This call to make disciples was not just about converting individuals; it was about fostering a community of believers who would continue to learn, grow, and follow Jesus' teachings. The Great Commission laid the groundwork for the early church, which became a community dedicated to fellowship, prayer, and the teaching of the apostles (Acts 2:42-47). The disciples took this commission seriously, traveling to distant lands, facing persecution, and even giving their lives to spread the Gospel.

- **7e. Love as the Defining Mark of Discipleship**

In His final instructions, Jesus emphasized the importance of love as the defining characteristic of His disciples. In John 13:34-35, He told them, "A new command I give you: Love one another. As I have loved you, so you must love one another. By this everyone will know that you are my disciples, if you love one another." This commandment to love was central to Jesus' teachings and mission.

Jesus' emphasis on love extended beyond personal affection; it was a sacrificial, unconditional love modeled after His own actions. This love was to be a witness to the world, setting His disciples apart from others. Their love for one another would reflect the unity and compassion of Christ, drawing others to the faith.

The disciples took this command to heart, building communities centered on love and mutual care. In Acts, we see the early church sharing their resources, supporting one another, and reaching out to those in need (Acts 4:32-35). This love became a powerful testimony to the world, attracting people to the Gospel not only through words but through the tangible example of a loving community.

- **7f. The Call to Persevere and Hold Fast to the Faith**

Jesus knew that His disciples would face trials and temptations that could weaken their faith. To prepare them, He encouraged them to hold fast to His teachings and remain steadfast. In John 15:4-5, He says, "Remain in me, as I also remain in you. No branch can bear fruit by itself; it must remain in the vine… apart from me you can do nothing." This call to abide in Him was a reminder of their dependence on God for strength, wisdom, and growth.

The metaphor of the vine and branches highlights the importance of staying connected to Christ as the source of life and vitality. By remaining in Him, the disciples would bear fruit—results that would last and have eternal significance. This lesson underscored that their success in ministry would not come from their own strength but from their relationship with Jesus.

The early church carried forward this lesson of perseverance. Despite persecution and trials, they held firm to their faith, encouraging one another to "stand firm" in the Lord (Philippians 4:1). This commitment to faith and perseverance became a hallmark of the Christian community, providing strength and resilience as they spread the Gospel in hostile environments.

- 7g. The Power of Prayer and Dependence on God

In His final teachings, Jesus demonstrated the importance of prayer as a means of connection with God and a source of strength. He modeled a life of prayer throughout His ministry, often retreating to quiet places to pray. In the Garden of Gethsemane, before His crucifixion, Jesus prayed fervently, submitting His will to the Father and seeking strength for what lay ahead (Matthew 26:36-39). This moment revealed His complete dependence on God and His willingness to obey, even at great personal cost.

Jesus taught His disciples to pray, encouraging them to bring their needs before God and trust in His provision. In John 14:13-14, He promises, "I will do whatever you ask in my name, so that the Father may be glorified in the Son." This promise assures them that God hears their prayers and responds to their faith. Prayer would become an essential part of the disciples'

Conclusion
The Legacy of a Master Teacher

The teachings and discipleship methods of Jesus Christ remain unparalleled in their depth, wisdom, and transformative power. By examining His approach, we have seen how Jesus masterfully combined instruction with relational guidance, modeling, questioning, empowerment, and practical application. His goal was not only to impart knowledge but to shape character, mold hearts, and invite His followers into a profound, life-altering relationship with God. Jesus' discipleship was about guiding people to become not merely students of His words, but embodiments of His message.

Each element of Jesus' teaching method reveals a different dimension of His wisdom as the Master Teacher. His modeling provided a living example of love, humility, and faith. His use of parables made deep truths accessible to everyone and invited listeners to reflect deeply. His questioning method fostered self-examination and encouraged a faith that is both personal and resilient. His empowerment of the disciples through practical ministry gave them confidence and independence, preparing them to spread His message to the ends of the earth. And finally, His final teachings centered on love, service, resilience, and the power of the Holy Spirit—qualities that would define the early church and inspire generations to come.

Jesus' method was as much about transformation as it was about information. He understood that true discipleship is a journey of the heart, mind, and soul—a process that requires commitment, reflection, and continual growth. He called His disciples to a path of humility, self-denial, and service, challenging them to step beyond cultural norms and embrace a radical, Kingdom-centered way of life. His teachings invited them to become more than followers; they were called to become messengers, representatives of God's love and truth in a broken world.

The legacy of Jesus' teaching continues to be relevant for modern discipleship. His example encourages today's believers to approach faith not merely as an academic pursuit or a set of beliefs, but as a way of life that impacts every relationship, every action, and every decision. Jesus' discipleship model reminds us that true faith goes beyond the surface, calling us into a life of purpose, compassion, and unwavering commitment to God.

As we reflect on Jesus' teachings and methods, we are challenged to consider our own discipleship journeys. Are we willing to follow in His footsteps, to live out His values, and to become conduits of His love and grace? Are we prepared to take His message to others, modeling a life that embodies His truth and serves as a beacon of hope to those around us?

The journey of discipleship is both an invitation and a responsibility. Jesus calls each of us to walk with Him, to learn from Him, and to reflect His light in a world that desperately needs it. His legacy as the Master Teacher is a reminder that the most effective teaching is not done through words alone, but through a life well-lived. May we take His example to heart, embracing the call to be true disciples and carrying His message forward with courage, humility, and love.

In following Jesus' discipleship model, we are not only growing closer to Him but also fulfilling the mission He entrusted to us: to be "the light of the world" (Matthew 5:14) and to make disciples of all nations. The Master Teacher has shown us the way—now, it is up to us to walk in it.

About the Author

Isaac Borson is a Preacher and student of historical and biblical teachings with a passion for exploring the profound impact of Jesus' life and methods. Inspired by a desire to make timeless lessons accessible and applicable to modern readers, Isaac Borson examines Jesus' discipleship method through a thoughtful, relatable lens.

The Master Teacher: Exploring the Discipleship Method of Jesus is a reflection of their commitment to bridging ancient wisdom with contemporary application, inviting readers to engage deeply with the teachings of Jesus in ways that touch both heart and mind.

Printed in Great Britain
by Amazon